MYTHS AND MONSTERS

GROWN-UP COLORING BOOK

VOLUME 1

WRITTEN AND ILLUSTRATED BY M. PATRICK DUGGAN

Published by Squid Black Entertainment
squidblack.com

Printed in the United States of America

10 9 8 7 6 5 4 3 2 1

MYTHS AND MONSTERS

GROWN-UP COLORING BOOK
VOLUME I

WRITTEN AND ILLUSTRATED BY M. PATRICK DUGGAN

Welcome to Myths & Monsters—hopefully the first of many Art Nouveau/Deco-styled coloring books by me. This book is homage to two of my favorite things: mythology and the Art Nouveau movement.

About the Mythology

Within these pages are goddesses, heroines, sorceresses, and monsters. They do not represent the sum total of mythical beings in history, of course—but a brief list I found interesting (or fun to draw). Many of them are from the distant past, while a few still have a modern place in some parts of the world. For that reason, I have attempted to be as respectful as possible, both in the illustrations and the writing (with a few infusions of humor).

About Art Nouveau

One of my favorite art movements, it was most popular between 1890 and 1910 (a pretty short time) before being replaced by Art Deco (another favorite, frankly) and then Modernism. It was a reaction to the previous academic art of the 19th century, and was greatly inspired by nature. My work in this book is a pale shadow of the geniuses who painted, built, sculpted, and led the original movement. But I hope you enjoy it anyway. If you are interested in learning more about Art Nouveau, I recommend you seek out the works of these nouveau masters: Alphonse Mucha, Gustav Klimt, Henri de Toulouse-Lautrec, Aubrey Beardsley, Virginia Frances Sterett, Koloman Moser, Walter Crane, Kay Nielsen, Jan Toorop, Stanislaw Wyspianski, Will H. Bradley, and Jules Cheret, just to name a few—or Google 'Art Nouveau Artists' if you're curious, and get ready to give your eyes a treat.

As a final note, if you enjoy this book, I hope you will write to me at ***mpatrickduggan.com*** and let me know? Also, if there are characters you'd like to see in a future edition, I'd love to hear your thoughts. Last, if you'd like to share your coloring of any of these pictures, I'd love to see them!

Thank you, and have a wonderful day.
M. Patrick Duggan

APHRODITE/VENUS

LOVE, BEAUTY, PLEASURE, AND PROCREATION (GREEK, ROMAN, AND PROBABLY MANY OTHERS)

Goddess on a mountain top, the summit of beauty and love... and Venus was her name.

This is one of the oldest legends in record. She is probably the most famous of the Greco-Roman gods, and to this day continues to be a metaphor. The idea of a force for love and romance persists in every culture on Earth.

VENUS • APHRODITE
MpDuggan

ARTEMIS/DIANA

THE HUNT, THE MOON, NATURE, AND BIRTH (GREEK, ROMAN, AND POSSIBLY MORE)

One of the most widely venerated goddesses of ancient Greece was Artemis. Mistress of animals and the wild, she was also affiliated with the moon, childbirth, and virginity. She was terribly beautiful, and several gods fell all over themselves for her. But she wasn't having any of that—as her only true love was Orion... but she may or may not have accidentally killed him on a hunting trip; or possibly her twin brother, Apollo, had him killed (that part was a little vague). There is also a story where Gaia (the earth mother) had him killed. Nobody but Artemis liked Orion, apparently. One way or the other, he wound up dead and Artemis stayed single. Another interesting thing about Artemis—she was beholden to no man, brilliant, and revered—in a time and place when women were losing their position in society. Contrast the legends of Hera (who had a cult far older) to Artemis, and you'll find striking differences. Why was Artemis still respected when Hera was clearly morphing into a neurotic?

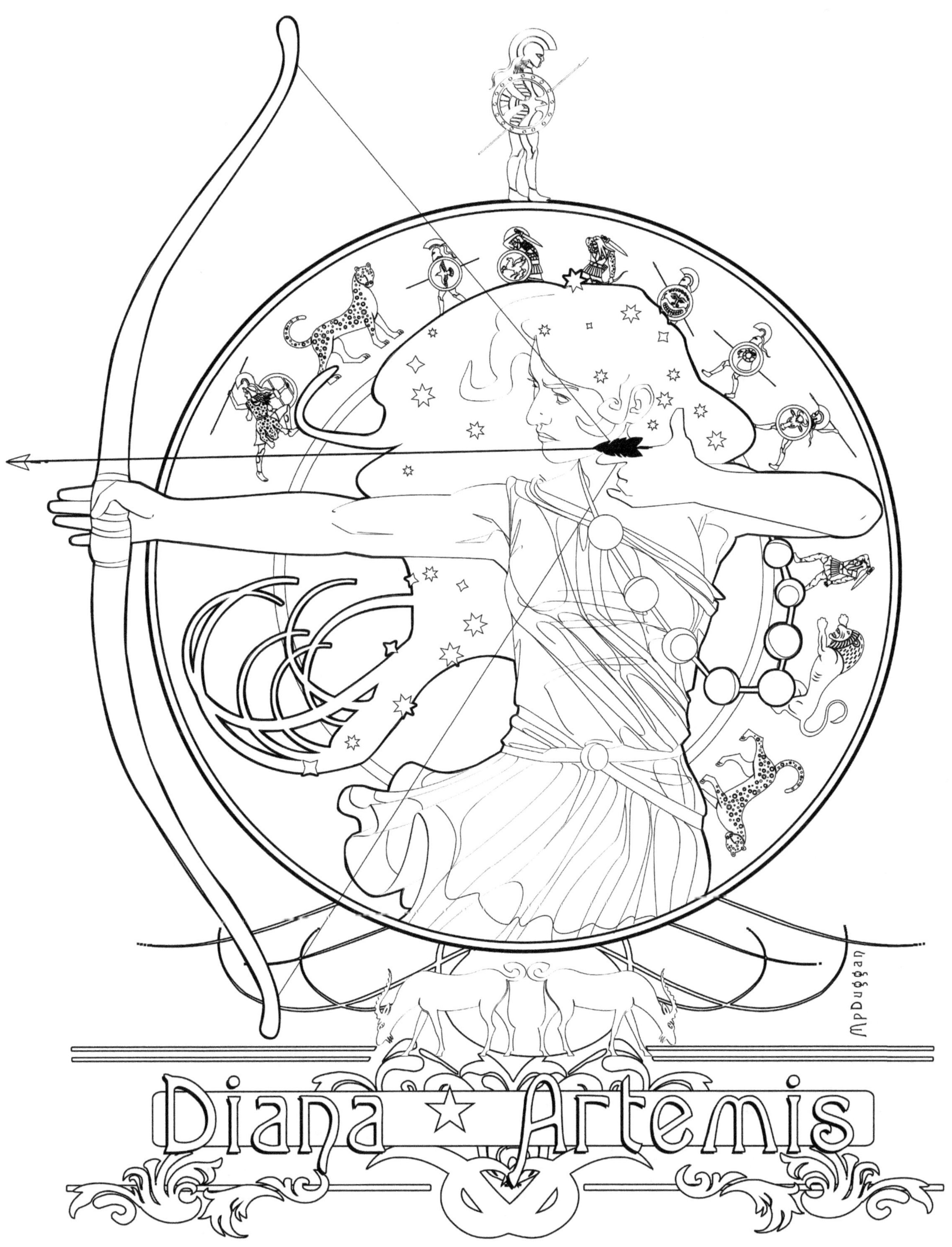
Diana ★ Artemis

BLUE CORN MAIDEN

SPRINGTIME AND KINDNESS (HOPI)

Corn Maidens figure into many Native American tribal mythologies. All of them are slightly different (Google 'corn maiden myth' and be prepared to be wowed). I heard the Hopi telling of the Blue Corn Maiden's story when I was a kid, and it always stuck with me.

Interestingly, I heard it before reading about Persephone (the Greek myth about the seasons), and was sure the Greeks stole the idea. Later, I was simply struck by the similarity. In a nutshell, Blue Corn Maiden was the nicest and kindest of the Corn Maidens, and she was super pretty. One day, Winter Katsina (a spirit of the earth) saw her and fell in love instantly. He invited her back to his place, and she kind of had to go with him, because to refuse would be rude—but then he froze everything around the house in permanent winter—and she was trapped there. At that point, Blue Corn Maiden was bummed, because she wanted to go home and help her people grow food (because she was nice, and weirdly, she wasn't scared, which is cool, because she's tough). But then Summer Katsina stumbles upon her and he gets into a fight with Winter Katsina and it's all a big problem.

Finally, they come to an agreement (they sat down over coffee, in a totally civilized Hopi way)—Blue Corn Maiden gets to go back to her people for half the year to help them grow food. The rest of the time, she hangs out with Winter Katsina—who, somewhere in this Beauty and the Beast story—turns out to be more than tolerable to her. And apparently it's all amicable.

Blue Corn Maiden
MpDuggan

BRAGI

POETRY
(NORSE)

Bragi is associated with bragr, the Norse word for poetry. The name of the god may have been derived from bragr, or the term bragr may mean 'what Bragi does'. A connection between Bragi and the bragarfull 'promise cup' is sometimes suggested, as bragafull, an alternate form of the word, might be translated as 'Bragi's cup'.

Bragi is thought to have been based on the historical ninth-century bard Bragi Boddason, whose poems were so artful, upon his death, Odin appointed him the court poet of Valhalla. It was a Norse parallel to sainthood. The Old Norse writers of the Christian Middle Ages took this a step further and actually portrayed Bragi as having been nothing less than a god of poetry all along. But there is no evidence he was ever worshipped, per se.

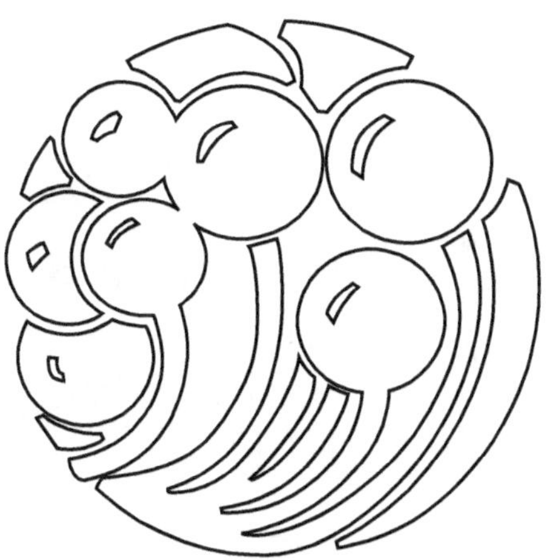

BRAGI

CYBELE

MOTHERS AND SOVEREIGNTY (PHRYGIAN, GREEK, ROMAN, AND POSSIBLY MORE)

Cybele's religion dates way back to ancient Phrygia (located in what is now central Turkey) and was imported to the Greek states around the 6th century BCE (a LONG time ago). She went on to become a very big deal with the Roman Empire, who called her 'Magna Mater' or mother goddess. She was interesting—and sort of stood beyond the core group of Greco-Roman/Olympian deities as an exotic foreign figure. Some scholars think she may have been a previous incarnation of Hera—before unification with the Olympian/Zeus/Apollo myths were used as a way to unify Greek society. The only problem with that theory is she showed up later as Cybele and came in as her own entity. The Romans also aligned her with the Trojans, and used that as a way to build credibility in their eastern provinces.

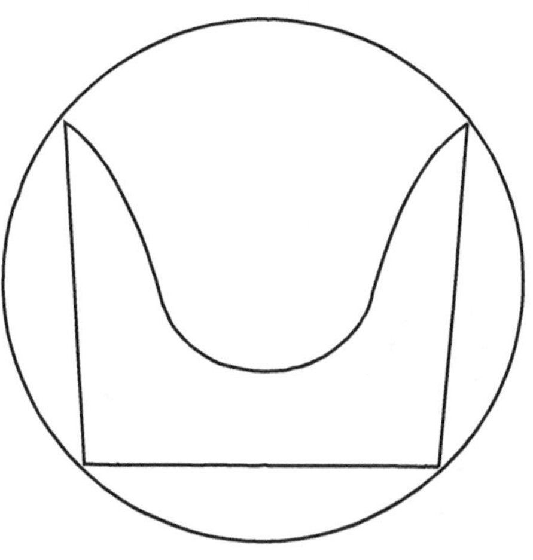

CYBELE

CYCLOPS

MONSTER
(GREEK, ROMAN)

Even though the term 'cyclops' actually means 'round-eyed' or 'circle of eyes'—we tend to think of this mythical monster as a one-eyed beast. However, there are several of them featured in Greek and Roman mythology—and they all appear to have a few traits in common: 1.) they are always some sort of giant, 2.) there's something going on with the eyes (one-eye, three-eyes, eyes across the body, etc), and 3.) they like to eat people.

CYCLOPS

DEMETER

AGRICULTURE, FERTILITY, AND THE HARVEST
(GREEK, MYCENEAN, ROMAN, AND POSSIBLY A FEW OTHERS)

Zeus, Aphrodite, and Apollo are all more famous, these days. But back in the ancient world, Demeter was a really big deal. She represented the harvest—essentially food. Though she is often described simply as the goddess of the harvest, she also presided over the cycle of life and death—and created the seasons. She and her daughter, Persephone, were the central figures of the Eleusinian Mysteries which predated the Olympian pantheon. Demeter is serious old school Indo-European, Indo-Mid East, Indo-whatever… her story crosses scores of cultures and incarnations. It might be time to hit Google, my friend.

D·E·M·E·T·E·R
MpDuggan

THE FATES

INCARNATIONS
(GREEK)

Also known as The Morai, the Fates were three sister deities who represented destiny and life. They were also in control of how long one might live, spinning the thread of time, and being generally very mysterious. Another thing about them: they didn't just control mortal fate—but also immortal... with the exception of Zeus. Strictly speaking, this might explain why Zeus was the boss—because the rest of his myths are pretty horrid.

the FATES

FRIGGA

FOREKNOWLEDGE AND WISDOM
(NORSE, OLD GERMAN, OLD ENGLISH, AND POSSIBLY OTHERS)

Wife of Odin and a great practitioner of magic, Frigga was the highest ranking Norse goddess. Despite that, very little is known about her. She may or may not have been Freyja—or some sort of composite from an older oral tradition which saw them as two sides of a coin. Many scholars think that the Frigga religion developed from something much older—something Scythian/Celtic that found its way into the Abyssinian world too. She might—if you will—be the same as Danu, Ishtar, pre-Olympian Hera, Cybele, and others.

FRIGGA

HARMONIA

PEACE, HARMONY, AND CONCORD (GREEK)

Harmonia was a daughter of Ares and Aphrodite. She presided over marital harmony (ironic, given she was the product of an affair) and soldiers in war. Some Greek and Roman writers portrayed her as harmony in a more abstract sense—cosmic balance. Either way, she must have been very laid-back. It wasn't all sunshine and flowers, though—when she got married to a fellow named Kadmos the king of Thebes, her horrid step-father Hephaistos (still mad at his wife for hooking up with the god of war) gave her a cursed necklace as a wedding gift... which doomed her descendants to unending tragedy. After a series of, yes, tragic setbacks, Harmonia and Kadmos moved to Illyria where they put down the locals and formed a new kingdom. Once that was settled, the gods showed up and turned everybody into snakes.

HARMONIA
MpDuggan

HERA

MARRIAGE, WOMEN, CHILDBIRTH, AND FAMILY (GREEK AND ROMAN)

Doesn't it seem like Hera got a bad rap?

First of all, she was the goddess of Marriage—but her own marriage was a mess. Her husband, Zeus, was completely impossible. Okay, first of all, she was his second wife… nothing wrong with that, of course—but only because he ate the first one. That should have been a red flag right there, right? He slept with everything that moved, was often very fussy about the weirdest things, and had tons of illegitimate kids everywhere. Between being consumed with jealousy and punishing people for sleeping with her husband (who could change shape and control mortal minds, so a lot of these people didn't even realize it was him, but ignorance is no excuse, right?) she had her hands full.

Doesn't it seem like scholarly revisionism? Some historians think Hera may have been based on an older Indo-European religion—one that was later molded to fit something more shrill and reactive. It may have been a way to integrate matrilineal regions around the Hellenistic world into a unified Greek culture.

HERA
MpDuggan

HORUS

THE SKY AND KINGSHIP (EGYPTIAN)

Horus is the god of the sky, and the son of Osiris, the creator. He was depicted as a falcon, or as a falcon-headed man. His name in Egyptian meant 'The Distant One'.

Horus was sometimes known as Nekheny (meaning falcon), although it has been proposed that Nekheny may have been another falcon-god, worshipped at Nekhen (city of the hawk) who became identified as Horus later. In this form, he was sometimes given the title Kemwer, meaning 'the great black one', referring to the bird's color.

HORUS

ICARUS

TRAGIC FIGURE (GREEK, ETRUSCAN)

Icarus' father Daedalus, a talented and remarkable Athenian craftsman, built the Labyrinth for King Minos of Crete near his palace at Knossos to imprison the Minotaur. Minos later imprisoned Daedalus in the labyrinth because he gave Minos's daughter, Ariadne, a clew (or ball of string) to help Theseus survive the Labyrinth and defeat the creature. Icarus was also imprisoned there. But Daedalus wasn't done. He fashioned two pairs of wings out of wax and feathers for himself and his son. Daedalus tried his wings first, but before trying to escape the island, he warned his son not to fly too close to the sun, nor fly too close to the sea—but follow his path of flight. Overcome by the giddiness of flying, Icarus soared into the sky, but he went too close to the sun—and the wax on his wings melted. Icarus kept flapping but soon realized he had no feathers left and fell to his death in the sea.

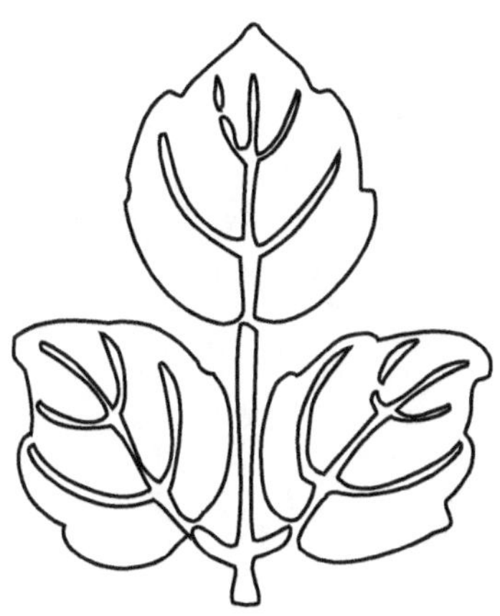

ICARUS
MpDuggan

ISIS

HEALTH, MARRIAGE, WISDOM, AND MAGIC
(EGYPTIAN, ROMAN, AND OTHERS)

Before lunatics recently ruined her name with an anagram, Isis was having a pretty good run. She started out as a fairly obscure deity. But as time went on, she became a huge presence in ancient Egypt. Her cult eventually spread to the Roman Empire where she was worshipped from England to Afghanistan—*for millenia*.

To this day, she is revered by certain pagans.

isis

KALI

TIME, CREATION, DESTRUCTION, AND POWER (HINDU AND BUDDHIST)

Nothing escapes the all-consuming march of time. Kali comes from the Sanskrit root word Kal which means time. Many think of her as a death goddess, but that is inaccurate. She is also considered a mother goddess in many places. Either way, her religion has stood the test of time, and looks like it will be sticking around.

Note about the picture—because this is a family-friendly book, I opted not to include the severed head and bowl of blood (not out of disrespect). But there's plenty of room there if you want to draw them in yourself.

KALI

THE KRAKEN

MONSTER
(GREEK, NORSE, AND OTHERS)

A legendary sea monster of gigantic size said to dwell off the coast of Norway—or possibly an incarnation of Ceto in Greek mythology? My version is a beautiful woman with tentacles. I'm trying something here. Hopefully, you like it and color it with every shade of green and blue in your arsenal!

The Kraken
MpDuggan

MACHA

WAR, HORSES, SOVEREIGNTY, AND ARMAGH (IRISH)

One of the sovereign goddesses of Ireland (her sisters were Badb and Morrigu), Macha is mostly associated with the region of Armagh. She has several legends, most relating to different women throughout the ages stepping in to save the realm in some way; many involving marrying kings who otherwise would have given up hope, or putting her foot down and saying something like, "Oh, we are NOT gonna take it!" There's an old Irish trope that reappears throughout writings—where a wise woman (the mother, the sister, the elderly aunt) suddenly appears and speaks common sense in some way—and thereby resets the family course. Macha may be a pre-metaphor for that.

Note about the picture—this piece is homage to the great artist, Alphonse Mucha. Sadly, my skills pale in comparison. But it was really fun to draw.

Macha
MpDuggan

MARDUK

THE SUN, OVERLORDSHIP, PATRON OF THE CITY OF BABYLON (MESOPOTAMIAN AND POSSIBLY OLDER)

This is one of those old-timey gods who morphed with the times. His religion appears to start deep in the Bronze Age of Sumeria—and grew over the centuries to dominate the Babylonian world. Whatever his original aspect (probably a sun god), his myth adapted to absorb other religions (see the Kingu/Tiamat reference where it is literally said he showed up and overthrew them) until he became the primary religious icon of the region. Marduk was almost certainly used as a unifying element (see Apollo for more on that) across several ancient cultures. In fact, he may have been a precursor to other sun gods across the Mediterranean and Asia Minor (including Apollo and Helios, and could even have been a pre-cursor to the Zeus mythology in some indirect way).
In short, this could be the guy who started it all with the idea of using church to affect state.

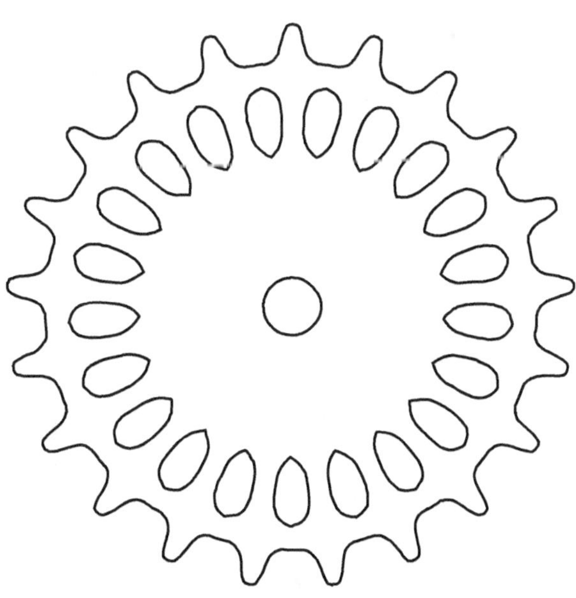

MARDUK
MpDuggan

MINOTAUR

MONSTER (MYCENEAN, MINOAN, GREEK, ROMAN)

King Minos prayed to Poseidon, the sea god, to send him a snow-white bull as a sign of support. The plan was to kill the bull to honor the deity, but Minos decided to keep it instead—because of it was pretty (I think we've all been there). He thought Poseidon would not care. But Poseidon did care (after all, what was the point, right?) As punishment, Poseidon made Minos's wife, Pasiphaë, fall in love with the bull. And love she did! She had the great craftsman Daedalus (see Icarus for more on him) make a hollow wooden cow, and climbed inside to mate with the creature. The offspring was the monstrous Minotaur. Pasiphaë nursed him, but as he grew he became ferocious (being the unnatural offspring of a woman and a beast). He also went around eating people. It was a mess. King Minos finally got Daedalus to construct a gigantic labyrinth to hold the Minotaur—and there it stayed until Theseus showed up and took care of business.

Minotaur

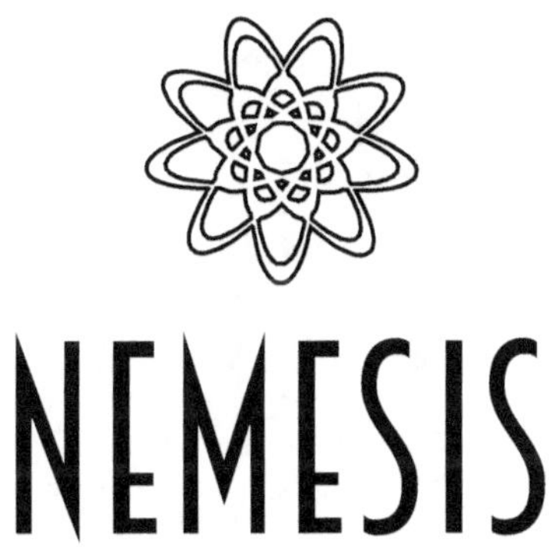

NEMESIS

RETRIBUTION
(GREEK AND ROMAN)

Nemesis was the goddess of retribution against those who succumb to hubris. One of the most famous stories involving her was the tale of Narcissus—who was some kind of incredibly handsome hunter guy living in the backwoods. He was so good-looking everybody just loved him. But he didn't have time for anyone else, because he was so taken with himself. Nemesis was not impressed. She lured him to a little pond where he saw his own reflection in a pool of water and fell in love with it. Unable to leave the beauty of his own reflection, Narcissus lost the will to live and basically starved.

The word Nemesis originally meant distributor of fortune, either good or bad, in proportion to what was deserved. Later, the word came to suggest a resentment caused by injustice, and the sense one could not allow it to pass unpunished. In the modern dialect, we often refer to this as 'karma'—but that is also inaccurate. The first time I remember hearing the word 'nemesis' was in high school—when one of my teachers referred to the 9-week summary grading period as her personal nemesis.

nemisis

NIKE

VICTORY (GREEK AND ROMAN)

In the ancient Greek religion, Nike was the personification of victory. Her Roman name was Victoria. I have a friend named Victoria—she cuts my hair and is brilliant, funny, and whimsical. Apparently the original wasn't so much. She was more of a drill sergeant, apparently. According to legend, she and her sisters hooked up with Zeus when he was planning to kill the Elder Titans, and then sort of became his cheerleaders who would fly around giving people congratulatory wreaths, blowing other people up, or just being very pro-Zeus.

NIKE

OKO

AGRICULTURE AND THE HARVEST (ORISHA OF WESTERN AFRICA)

Oko holds the secrets of farming and the harvest—maintaining the stability of life. He's a very fair-minded spirit, and dislikes arguments. He is also the first one to jump to any female's defense. Oko's worshippers would also petition him for prosperity, good fortune, and health.

OKO

PROTEUS

PRIMORDIAL – THE SEAS, RIVERS (GREEK)

One of the early sea gods of Greek mythology, Proteus governed rivers and smaller sea areas (he wasn't an executive like Poseidon, apparently—more like middle management). He was also very shape-changery, and represented the aspect of water constantly shifting.

Fun Trivia: Homer called him the 'Old Man of the Sea', and he's popped up in all kinds of literature over the centuries.

PROTEUS
MPDuggan

PSYCHE

THE SOUL
(GREEK AND ROMAN)

She was once a mortal princess whose extraordinary beauty earned the ire of Aphrodite (who apparently didn't like competition) when men began turning their worship away from the goddess towards the girl. Aphrodite commanded Eros to make Psyche fall in love with the most hideous of men. But he took one look at her and fell in love himself. Eros hid his true identity (because he's kind of a moron) and told her she must never gaze upon his face (because that's reasonable, right?). BUT THEN her sisters got jealous—and they tricked her into disobeying (or maybe they were like, 'dude, your new beau, he looks like a baby with wings'). So Eros took a nutty and forsook her. Despite the fact that he was clearly a hot mess, she searched the world for him and eventually came back into the service of Aphrodite—who clearly forgot about the earlier ire business.

The goddess commanded her to perform a series of seemingly impossible tasks (which she totally crushed) which culminated in a journey to the Underworld (Hecate hopped in at one point and hopefully reminded her that Eros isn't worth it, but whatever, and I suspect there was a musical number somewhere). Psyche was reunited with Eros and the couple were married in a ceremony attended by all the gods.

psyche
MpDuggan

PTAH

CREATION, THE ARTS, FERTILITY AND CRAFTSMEN (EGYPTIAN)

Ptah was one of the big creator gods of the ancient Egyptians, and dates back well before 400 BCE. Unlike most of the other Egyptian gods, he doesn't appear to waste much time fighting and scheming—but rather looks to have been a very steady fellow.

Ptah

QUAN YIN

COMPASSION AND MERCY
(CHINESE, JAPANESE, KOREAN, AND BUDDHIST)

One of the deities most frequently seen on altars in China's temples is Quan Yin (also spelled Kwan Yin, Kuanyin, and Guanyin). In Sanskrit, her name is Padma-pâni, or "Born of the Lotus." Quan Yin, alone among Buddhist gods, is loved rather than feared. The name Kuan Shih Yin, as she is often called, means literally, "The one who regards, looks on, or hears the sounds of the world."

According to legend, she was about to enter heaven but paused on the threshold as the cries of the world reached her ears.

QUAN
YIN
MpDuggan

SPIDER GRANDMOTHER

CREATION
(HOPI AND NATIVE AMERICAN)

According to several Native American oral traditions, Spider Grandmother was the creator of the entire world. After that, she went around teaching people, helping, and being generally awesome.

The story I heard, as a child, goes like this: she took a web and threw it at the sky.

When it stuck, she gathered drops of dew and hurled them too.

When they caught the webs, we had the stars.

SPIDER GRANDMOTHER
MpDuggan

THANATOS

DEATH
(GREEK)

Thanatos was the Greek god of Death. Unlike his Roman counterpart, Mors, he was slightly more specific—he represented non-violent death (violent death was something the rest of the Olympians could handle on their own), because his touch was 'gentle'. Ironically, the Greeks always depicted him as rather… sexy. I'm not sure what that's about. But there, I said it.

THANATOS

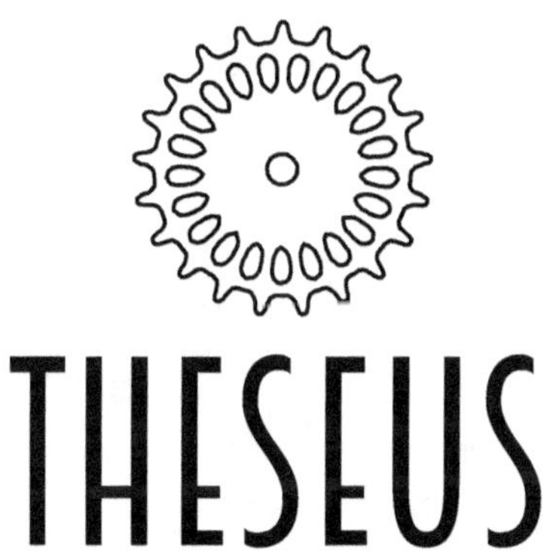

THESEUS

HERO
(GREEK)

The great hero Theseus comes from Attic legend. He was the son of either the king of Athens or Poseidon the sea god (depending on the source material). When Theseus reached adulthood, his mother sent him to Athens to find his destiny. Along the way, he had many adventures—killing the Sinis at the Isthmus of Corinth, then the Crommyonian sow, the wicked Sciron, Procrustes (who was basically a crazy man), and Cercyon (a hot-head who insisted on wrestling everybody). Once he got to Athens, his father (the king of Athens this time, not the sea god) was married to the sorceress Medea (who has her own totally nutty back-story). She tried to have him poisoned, but it backfired. After that, Theseus basically went on tour—killing fire-breathing bulls, the Minotaur, and sort of re-formed the country a bit. The adventures didn't stop there—he even went to the underworld for a while.

Theseus

ZEUS

THE SKY, LIGHTNING, THUNDER, LAW, ORDER AND JUSTICE (GREEK, ROMAN)

Zeus (or Jupiter in the Roman myth) was the primary god of the sky and ruler of the Olympian pantheon. He overthrew his father, Cronus the Titan, and drew lots with his brothers Poseidon and Hades, to decide who would succeed the throne. Zeus won the draw and became the supreme ruler of the gods. His weapon was a thunderbolt which he hurled at anyone who displeased him, especially liars and oath-breakers—which is ironic... as he was married to Hera but was infamous for his many affairs.

Zeus, the presiding deity of the universe, ruler of the skies and the earth, was regarded by the Greeks as the god of all natural phenomena above; the personification of the laws of nature; the ruler of the state; and finally, the father of gods and men.

ZEUS - JUPITER
MpDuggan

M. PATRICK DUGGAN

M. Patrick Duggan is a writer and cartoonist.

He has worked as an illustrator, colorist, or writer on several comic books, magazines, and novels–including Disney Adventures, The Tick, Foodang, The Dark, Green Lantern, Fantastic Four, Clown With A Gun, The Lemming, Bunny & Turtle, The Man Named Elinor, NUOS, Atomic Clown, Atomic Men, and LA: Heaven and Hell–and drawn storyboards for The Tick, DinoTrux, Doug, King of the Hill, Astrid Strudelman, and The Wild Thornberries. In addition, he has drawn many merchandising pieces from trading cards to toy cover artwork for major franchises, including Harry Potter, DC Comics Heroes, and more.

M. Patrick is a proud nerd with profound opinions about Art Nouveau, Art Deco, Mythology, Star Wars, Star Trek, Battlestar Galactica, and... yes... The West Wing. Rumor has it the Sorting Hat put him in Hufflepuff. He's not sure what to think about that.

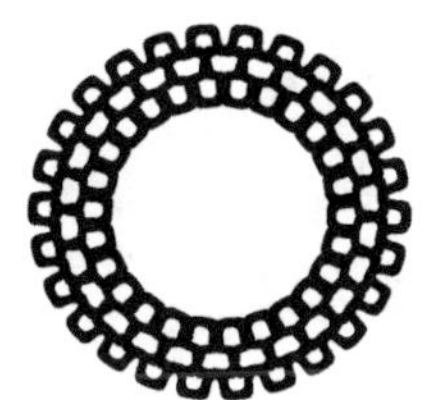

THANK YOU

Writing (and drawing) a book is never really done alone--friends and family are often called-upon for moral (and sometimes financial) support. There are editors, and all kinds of other people involved. To those people, I cannot thank you enough for your endless patience, support, and goodwill. Also, I'd like to include a list of specific people who gave advice and/or extra encouragment (if I forget someone, please forgive me): Alan Pierce, Rachel Fain, Nina Mahdavi, John & Virginia Duggan, Joseph Naftali, Alexandrea Weis, Liana Gardner, Dixie De La Tour, Linda Bailey Walsh, Sam Shearon, and my Literary Agent, Italia Gandolfo.

RESOURCES

If you'd like to learn more about Mythology, Art Nouveau, or Adult Coloring Books--here are just a few excellent resources:

MYTHOLOGY

Irish Folk & Fairytale Omnibus by Michael Scott
An Encyclopedia of Faeries by Katharine Briggs
The Odyssey by Homer
The Iliad by Homer
Mythology: Times Tales of Gods and Heroes by Edith Hamilton
The Power of Myth by Joseph Campbell

ART NOUVEAU

Alphonse Mucha by Sarah Mucha
Gustav Klimt and Egon Schiele by Simon R. Guggenheim Museum
Art Nouveau by Robert Schmutzler
Art Nouveau: The Style of the 1890s by Francesco Abbate
Art Nouveau (The Colour Library of Art) by Martin Battersby

ADULT COLORING BOOKS

coloringbookaddict.com
thecoloringbookclub.com
coloringclub.com
coloringqueen.net
inkspirations.com

www.ingramcontent.com/pod-product-compliance
Lightning Source LLC
LaVergne TN
LVHW080018110826
845148LV00020B/1201